32

The reverential fear of the Lord

> "The [reverent] fear of the Lord [that is, worshiping Him and regarding Him as truly awesome] is the beginning and the preeminent part of knowledge [its starting point and its essence]; But arrogant fools despise [skillful and godly] wisdom and instruction and self-discipline."
>
> PROVERBS 1:7 *AMP*

Reverent, respect, honor

Having reverential fear of the Lord sounded unappealing to me. I didn't understand it. I thought wow, that sounds like something I don't want to sign up for. I lived life my way, I sinned, I lived in my own carnal knowledge. I always say sinning is fun until it's NOT. I loved doing things my way because I loved control.

As you see in this passage, I was labeled a fool. Who wants to be labeled as a fool? That day, I read this scripture in a new way. That day, I chose to give up myself and chose to fear the Lord. Wow, what a day.

The fear of the Lord means you respect and honor Him. It means you choose to serve Him and not the things of this world. Is it still hard some days? Of course. The fear of the Lord is the beginning of knowledge. Seek Him and let Him direct your ways. Put your hope, confidence and trust in Him. This is the starting point to a much, much better way.

Are you full of knowledge and wisdom fearing the Lord?

How can you choose to seek Him instead of yourself and the worlds way?

How do you think honoring the Lord blesses you?

_____

_____

_____

_____

_____

_____

_____

_____

_____

I pray if this is your first-time yearning to really choose to fear the Lord, He comes with love and truth as you seek Him. I believe you will be blessed abundantly.

33

Are you living as a fool or choosing victory?

> "Where there is no [wise, intelligent] guidance, the people fall [and go off course like a ship without a helm], But in the abundance of [wise and godly] counselors there is victory."
>
> PROVERBS 11:14 *AMP*

Fool, mislead

Victory, triumph, success, advantage, prosperity

I said before, this isn't always easy. It's a lifestyle change. It's going against the world and its ways. We live in this world, so it takes being intent in the word, and daily, sometimes hourly,

55 DAYS

Seeking Him

Lacey Whittaker

Edited by Lil Barcaski and Justin Whittaker

Published by: GWN Publishing
www.GWNPublishing.com

Cover Design: Kristina Conatser | Captured by KC Designs
www.capturedbykcdesigns.com

ISBN: 978-1-959608-02-8

Dedication

To all those devotional lovers. I had so much fun writing this one. This book is something I want to read and engage in myself again and again. I hope you will feel the same way!

Introduction

Seek Him. This book is a collective of 55 days of devotions with enough room to write your own thoughts and answer questions for yourself. I too find myself working through these same questions. The book will take you through His will over ours, the gifts of the spirit, the fruits of the spirit and so much more.

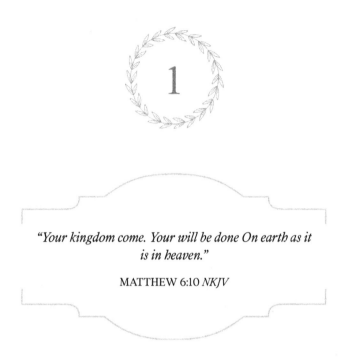

1

"Your kingdom come. Your will be done On earth as it is in heaven."

MATTHEW 6:10 *NKJV*

Lord, Your will is what we want. Your eyes to see. Your ears to hear. Your mouth to speak. We ask for all of this, Lord. We simply will not miss when our heart is directed towards You. When our minds are focused on truth. Lord, give us all these things forever and ever. You will reign!

How many times do you state this verse? How many times do you believe and live this verse? This verse is so important. As we live in this fallen world, our heart should be set on truth. We should wake up saying, Lord, not my will but Yours be done. It's a daily, hourly, sometimes by minute, surrender.

Why do you think this is hard to do most days?

_____

_____

_____

_____

_____

_____

_____

How do you get His eyes to see? His ears to hear? His words to speak?

_____

_____

_____

_____

_____

_____

_____

How can you be more intent in living this way?

_____

_____

_____

_____

_____

_____

_____

2

> *"But let him who glories glory in this, That he understands and knows Me, That I am the Lord, exercising loving kindness, judgment, and righteousness in the earth. For in these I delight," says the Lord."*
>
> JEREMIAH 9:24 *NKJV*

I remember the day, not many years ago, when this verse would've seemed foreign to me. Like I know of God, but I don't really know Him. I didn't know I could really have a relationship with Him. I grew up in church. I guess I didn't get the memo. I guess it went over my head. I guess I was stuck in religion instead. The day I got this, it changed my life. It changed everything. Was it easy to get there? No. It wasn't easy at all. I had to fight to get there. I had to fight the distractions. I had to fight the selfish life I knew. I had to fight and choose not to lose. I had to make the time to sit. Oh, this was hard. It was pitiful. I could barely sit in silence for a minute. I would tuck away to pray. This took me many days to even feel comfortable sitting. When I did, I caught a thought one day, and after that, I never wanted to give that precious time away. He speaks and He yearns for that one-on-one relationship with you. Sit and ask Him to speak and start fresh, anew.

How can you make time today to sit with Him?

_____

_____

_____

_____

_____

_____

_____

How will you cancel out the distractions?

_____

_____

_____

_____

_____

_____

Don't be hard on yourself, give yourself time. Don't give up.

Start by setting a timer for a minute or five and just sit with Him in silence. This will change your whole world.

3

"Give thanks to the Lord and proclaim his greatness. Let the whole world know what he has done. Sing to Him; yes, sing His praises. Tell everyone about His wonderful deeds. Exult in His holy name; rejoice, you who worship the Lord. Search for the Lord and for his strength; continually seek Him. Remember the wonders He has performed, His miracles, and the rulings He has given,"

1 CHRONICLES 16:8-12 *NLT*

Once you know Him, it's your heart's desire to seek Him. Once you know Him, you want to share Him. Once you know Him, you want to worship Him. Search Him, praise Him, thank Him for His all-mighty goodness. This takes being intent. Yes, the desire is there, but also the distraction, the kids, the things to do, the wondering if they will persecute you. So, choose today, there will be no other way. Choose to be intent and live in His grace and forgiveness. Choose Him. Live your life pursuing, seeking, sharing His love for all, and your purpose will flourish. That's our call.

What are some ways you seek Him?

_____

_____

_____

_____

_____

After your time seeking Him, how do you feel?

_____

_____

_____

_____

_____

How do you feel when you let days or weeks go by and you chose not to be intent?

_____

_____

_____

_____

_____

If this is new to you, start by waking up and thanking Him.

Talk to Him throughout your day and see the change.

Lord, I love you. Thank you for leading me today. Thank you for going before me and never leaving.

4

"But all that is recorded here is so that you will fully
believe that Jesus is the Anointed One, the Son of God,
and that through your faith in Him you will experience eternal life by the power of His name!"

JOHN 20:31 *TPT*

Jesus. Such a precious name. He died to save. A friend like no
other. A teacher. He loves the unlovable. Words could never
fully describe the love I feel for Him. He sees us and loves us
until the very end. I went three decades without calling His
name! Now, I live every day to praise His name. I live every day
to honor Him and obey.

✳ *What kind of relationship do you have with Jesus?*

_____

_____

_____

_____

How can you make it stronger?

_____

_____

_____

_____

_____

_____

_____

How do you share Jesus with others?

_____

_____

_____

_____

_____

_____

_____

Today, if you don't have this relationship, I pray you ask Him for one. Repent, surrender. and call on Jesus' name.

Jesus, Jesus, precious holy one. Jesus, Jesus, You are the only one that makes my heart love so deep. Jesus, oh Jesus, I feel when You weep. Jesus, oh Jesus, You are so kind. Jesus, oh Jesus, and the best friend of mine. Jesus, oh Jesus, I think of what I could've missed if I never said I love You and You are worth all of it. Jesus, oh Jesus, You chose me first. Jesus, oh Jesus, that's my worth. Jesus, oh Jesus, You are so kind. Jesus, oh Jesus, forever mine.

5

"And I will ask the Father and He will give you
another Savior, the Holy Spirit of Truth, who will be
to you a friend just like me—and He will never leave
you. The world won't receive Him because they can't
see Him or know Him. But you know Him intimately
because He remains with you and will live inside you."

JOHN 14:16-17 TPT

When Jesus left us, He left us with something greater. He left
the Holy Spirit to anyone that is a Christ follower. The Holy
Spirit lives in you and remains there. The Holy Spirit shows
us how to encounter Jesus. He shows us how to live and pray.
He is our great intercessor. He is our helper and our friend.
He shows us truth. He warns of trouble. He never leaves us.
He is a person. I went most of my life not knowing this. I have
heard Father, Son, Holy Spirit maybe 300 times. I didn't know
the role or the power until a few years ago. When that power
came over me, I was floored. I was thankful and yearning for
more. How could this be? I wanted the encounters desperately.
Now, I'm deeper in my journey and I can't imagine a day
that would go by without me leaning in to hear, discern,

edify, encourage, lead, and feed me. The Holy Spirit is the best thing Jesus gave me.

What words would you use to describe the Holy Spirit?

_____
_____
_____
_____
_____

How has He nudged you or taught you?

_____
_____
_____
_____
_____

Do you consider Him your friend?

_____
_____
_____
_____
_____

Maybe you don't know how to get this relationship. Ask Jesus today to make the Holy Spirit known to you and thank Him for living inside of you.

You are my helper, my friend, the one that comforts and knows no end. You are my joy, my light, the one that always provides. You are my shelter when I need to hide. You are my forever lifted high. You are my everything inside of me. You are the air I breathe. Thank you, Holy Spirit, for finding a home in me. Thank you, Father, for I cannot imagine life without Thee.

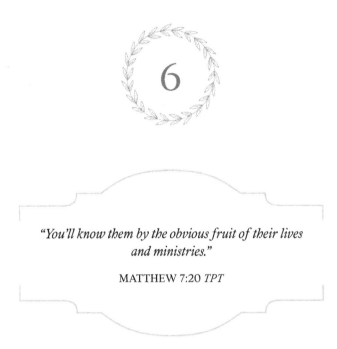

6

"You'll know them by the obvious fruit of their lives
and ministries."

MATTHEW 7:20 *TPT*

He calls us to bear fruit. To remain in the vine, to be pruned. He calls us to bear much fruit. There have been seasons in my life when I thought I was bearing good fruit, but I was not. I was not walking in what God had called me to. I was walking my will, my way doing lots of good things, so I thought. I was tired, and running, serving, and pouring. No fruit was bore. Sometimes this can be deceiving. As we live in the world and see many things, we must ask the Lord what His will is, not ours. We must walk in what He has for us.

❋ What does your fruit produce?

_____

_____

_____

_____

_____

❋ Is it the fruit God has touched?

_____

_____

_____

_____

_____

❋ Is there rotten fruit in your life that may be disguised?

_____

_____

_____

_____

_____

Ask the Lord today to look inside and show you the way.

Pruning. Pruning is what you do to bear, to bear much juicy fruit. Pruning, as hard as it can be, I know how wonderfully well it is for me. Prune this pride and insecurity. Prune it, so I can leave it all lay at Your feet. Soar above this fruit. I shall eat. Prune, oh Father, prune. For my will is only to be used by You.

7

> *"But the fruit of the Spirit [the result of His presence
> within us] is love [unselfish concern for others], joy,
> [inner] peace, patience [not the ability to wait, but
> how we act while waiting], kindness, goodness, faith-
> fulness, gentleness, self-control. Against such things
> there is no law."*

GALATIANS 5:22-23 *AMP*

Today, sit and pray on these things. Go to your Bible and search
each fruit. I love to use my thesaurus too. I love to look up the
word and see how it applies to me. Sit and seek these fruits. We
will dive into each one in the next days to come.

*Love • Joy • Peace • Patience • Kindness • Goodness
Faithfulness • Gentleness • Self-Control*

8

Love

> "Those who are loved by God, let his love continually pour from you to one another, because God is love. Everyone who loves is fathered by God and experiences an intimate knowledge of Him. The one who doesn't love has yet to know God, for God is love. The light of God's love shined within us when He sent His matchless Son into the world so that we might live through Him. This is love: He loved us long before we loved Him. It was His love, not ours. He proved it by sending His Son to be the pleasing sacrificial offering to take away our sins. Delightfully loved ones, if He loved us with such tremendous love, then "loving one another" should be our way of life!"

1 JOHN 4:7-11 *TPT*

Love, passion, adoration, devotion, beloved,
cherish, desire

God loves us. He loved us first. He sent His Son to die for us. What greater love is this? He has called us to love one another. It sounds like an easy thing to do really when you read these words, He left us with. Especially knowing all He gave and all He did. Knowing He loves us in the thick of our sin. He loves us even when we turn against.

How do you love? How do you love the unlovable? It seems when people come against me, it's easy to forget what He has asked of me. Instead, I want what's best for me. Today, I ask for His love to be still, to run through and always be well. I ask to be humble and love others at their worst because really that's how our Father shows His love for us when we run off course.

How do you feel Gods love?

_____

_____

_____

_____

_____

_____

_____

_____

_____

_____

※ *How do you love the unlovable?*

_____

_____

_____

_____

_____

_____

_____

_____

_____

※ *Are there any things you can change to love as the Father has asked us to love?*

_____

_____

_____

_____

_____

_____

_____

_____

_____

9

Joy

> "Daily, I will worship You passionately and with all my heart. My arms will wave to You like banners of praise. I overflow with praise when I come before You, for the anointing of Your presence satisfies me like nothing else. You are such a rich banquet of pleasure to my soul. I lie awake each night thinking of You and reflecting on how You help me like a father. I sing through the night under Your splendor-shadow, offering up to You my songs of delight and joy!"
>
> PSALMS 63:4-7 *TPT*

Joy, delight, gladness, rejoice, blessedness, supernatural strength

Joy comes from God. His presence brings me joy. A word, healing, miracle, answered prayer. Hearing Him say, I am with you in this trial, this battle of your life, this wayward child, I am with you. The joy of the Lord is my strength. It comes on when I need Him with everything. It comes in the good and the bad. This joy I shall forever have. Try and find joy in all things. Find joy and let freedom ring.

What brings you joy?

_____

_____

_____

_____

_____

_____

_____

Do you feel joy in your deepest pain?

_____

_____

_____

_____

_____

_____

_____

Ask God to give you joy today.

10

Peace

> "Be anxious for nothing, but in everything by prayer
> and supplication, with thanksgiving, let your requests
> be made known to God; and the peace of God, which
> surpasses all understanding, will guard your hearts
> and minds through Christ Jesus."
>
> PHILIPPIANS 4:6-7 *NKJV*

Peace, calm, stillness, ease, rest

The opposite of peace is known as war, mental stress, anxiety, fear, and worry. You may be thinking, war? I think of the war inside of me that festers up in my heart and mind. If I don't guard my heart and mind, I let in stress, bad thoughts, and a hard heart. I then reap anxiety, fear, and worry. One time, I had let it go so far out of control that I was having panic attacks for months. I couldn't eat, I couldn't sleep, I couldn't care for my

2-year-old daughter. I was a mess. I was getting daily radiation treatments and one day I snapped! I spent a good six months trying to recover. The only thing that helped was saying, Jesus. I probably said it 1,000 times. I then sat down and meditated on scripture, I tried to think good thoughts. It was a long process, but the Lord was healing me slowly, teaching me how to let go and depend on Him. Ten years later, I don't go many days a year feeling a lack of peace. I know my source. I know what I need to do. I know peace and my peace now is everything to me. Pray, and thank Him until the peace floods you!

Do you find it hard to live in peace?

_____

_____

_____

_____

_____

_____

_____

What steals your peace?

_____

_____

_____

_____

_____

_____

_____

_____

What can you do to be intent to get into peace and live there?

Sit and quietly say Jesus, Jesus, Jesus, over and over until you feel peace.

11

Patience

> "Therefore, as the elect of God, holy and beloved, put on tender mercies, kindness, humility, meekness, long-suffering; bearing with one another, and forgiving one another, if anyone has a complaint against another; even as Christ forgave you, so you also must do. But above all these things put on love, which is the bond of perfection. And let the peace of God rule in your hearts, to which also you were called in one body; and be thankful."
>
> COLOSSIANS 3:12-15 *NKJV*

Patience, long suffering

One day, I asked the Lord to help me be patient. Why, I don't know? Really, I probably won't ask for that ever again. It was miserable. I want all the fruits, but patience, you and I have a hard time! I read it's called the tolerance of delay. We live in a world of the here and now, fast pace, did I mention we want everything right now this very minute? I get on Amazon and it's here in two days. But what about those things you wait on? How about those, wait upon the Lord times? Those hit differently. Those are more fulfilling. Waiting on a dream, being patient at work when your boss continually looks over you or showing mercy to angry people. You are bearing with another, you are forgiving, you are showing love and mercy. When I choose to do it His way, I come out stronger in endurance. I have peace in growth. I feel loved and known by our creator.

How can you be more patient today?

_____

_____

_____

_____

_____

_____

_____

Are you willing to ask Him to help you be patient?

_____

_____

_____

_____

_____

_____

_____

Why is it better to be patient than not?

_____

_____

_____

_____

_____

_____

_____

_____

Wait on the Lord. Have courage. Be of good cheer. He has His timing. He has His plan. He will strengthen you in the waiting if you choose to draw near. To walk in patience and peace. To walk and say, Lord I shall wait.

12

Kindness

> "Be kind and helpful to one another, tender-hearted
> [compassionate, understanding], forgiving one another
> [readily and freely], just as God in Christ
> also forgave you."
>
> EPHESIANS 4:32 *AMP*

*Kindness, compassion, generosity, goodwill,
grace, mercy, understanding, unselfish*

Jesus calls us to be kind. I feel like I am a kind person. I love to do things for others. I love to encourage and build up my family and friends. What I have a hard time with is the unlovable ones. I guess they just hit my flesh all wrong. I may start out loving them but then I find myself being harsh and cold. I don't really feel like being kind in those situations. Jesus called us to be kind to everyone. This is something I need Him to help me with in those situations. What about selfishness? I don't consider myself selfish.

This week I had to repent. I had to tell Jesus and my tribe I was sorry. It was me, my dreams, my ways, my everything. I was disappointed and hurt. That left me bitter and selfish. The first thing I did was acknowledge. The second thing I did was tell them I was sorry. The third thing was telling them I was grateful for them. Lastly, I bought my auntie some glasses she needed help with trying to find. After two hours, I felt so much better because I was thinking of others and not myself. Don't be hard on yourself when this does happen. I think little things we don't keep in check will get us here quick. Have a repentant heart and do good!

How do you feel you show your kindness?

_____

_____

_____

_____

_____

_____

How can you be better in hard situations?

_____

_____

_____

_____

_____

_____

Try and do an act of kindness a day for 10 days. See how you feel after those 10 days. It could be a word of encouragement, an act of service, or reaching out and praying with someone in need. Generosity will never leave you empty.

13

Goodness

Goodness, kindness, honesty, love, generosity

Oh, the goodness of God. How we long for the goodness of God. How He loves to give His children all good things. He loves to pour out for all to see. He is so good. Look around; His creation is so beautiful and magnificent. Sit in nature and thank Him for this goodness. Trust His goodness. His plan. Do not be overcome by evil but do good. Be kind. Lend a hand. Be a person of honesty. Love at all times. This love covers a multitude of sins. Yes, there is evil all around us, but choose the goodness, the fullness, the righteousness of God. You will be well rewarded. You will be blessed.

Look around, taste and see what is good. Name five things God has shown you as good.

_____

_____

_____

_____

_____

_____

_____

What about the bad things in your life? How can you overcome these things with His goodness?

_____

_____

_____

_____

_____

_____

_____

Maybe you never felt you have experienced His true goodness. Pray these words below over and over.

Souls you save. Souls you keep. Souls like mine. We love to reap all Your goodness, all You share. Jesus, Holy Spirit, You are welcome here. Come, Holy Spirit, flood through me. Pour your cup over me. Jesus, I look up and see only Your goodness and everlasting glory.

14

Faithfulness

Faithfulness, loyal, devoted, steadfast, faith

God is faithful and just. I feel it, I know it. I believe He will always be, no matter what. He is faithful. What hurts is when that friend you never thought would leave you, betrays you. Leaves and never looks back. That family member that constantly talks behind your back. That son or daughter that decides to up and leave and screams defeat. All those you have sown into, only to just up and leave you. All those you have sown into, what a mighty blow. I have to say, Lord help me let go of that deep pain, as I know You were betrayed and beat. Help me forgive and live faithful as You are to me. Help me see You are all I truly need.

Do you know God is faithful?

_____
_____
_____
_____
_____
_____

Write 5 ways you see His faithfulness daily.

_____
_____
_____
_____
_____
_____

Have you felt betrayal?

_____
_____
_____
_____
_____
_____

How can you fully let go of that betrayal now knowing our Lord is always faithful and asks us to forgive them?

15

Gentleness

> *"Let your gentleness be evident to all. The Lord is near."*
>
> PHILIPPIANS 4:5 *NIV*

Gentleness, compassion, mercy, meekness, kindness

The opposite of gentleness screams aggressive, pushy, harsh. How many times have you gone to a dear friend or family member looking for a gentle answer and they have come back screaming harsh words or advice telling you are not right? How many times were you the one that did the same to them? I feel I can be an aggressive person and would've more than likely been the one coming at you like this. Since my relationship with Jesus has grown and gone deeper, I learned His gentle ways, His gentle answers, His gentle, kind, and mercy overflowing upon me when I needed it the most. I learned a new way. I learned to be a good friend, a good mom, a good daughter. I would have to sit, listen, and be gentle. It takes time, being intent, and Jesus living within. To be gentle is to be grace. Choose to live like this today and see the change.

Are you a gentle person?

_____

_____

_____

_____

If not, how can you choose to be more gentle?

_____

_____

_____

_____

_____

_____

Do you believe Jesus wants us to be gentle at all times?

_____

_____

_____

_____

_____

Gentleness and compassion go hand and hand. Learn to have compassion on all of them.

16

Self-Control

> *"If you live without restraint and are unable to
> control your temper, you're as helpless as a city with
> broken-down defenses, open to attack."*
>
> PROVERBS 25:28 *TPT*

Self-control, restraint

He gives us freedom to live as we choose. He tells us what is good and bad. He tells us to not look back. He shows us His ways. He teaches us to follow and obey. Seek His word and pray. That can be easy for many things. What about the hard things? What about those things where you lose your self control? For me it's food. I use it as comfort. What about exercise, or lack of I should say? What about that relationship that makes you explode every time? What about that sin you choose time and time again? We all have our battles with self-control. How do you handle these things you try to hold? Do you try and control? I think that's the problem. When we try to control these things and not allow the Holy Spirit to rise within us on these hard things, govern us, teach us, be the one that breaks us free from these insecurities that we have felt so deep, for so long. Sometimes we get so comfortable in the things not good for us that we would rather stay there than grow in what's best for us. Let the Holy Spirit in you do a new thing. Let go of your control and let this fruit grow and show.

What are some things you have a hard time with self-control?

_____

_____

_____

_____

_____

_____

Do you feel it's almost impossible to overcome these things?

_____

_____

_____

_____

_____

_____

Ask the Holy Spirit to help you today. Be gentle with yourself.

I believe in repentance and freedom in Jesus' name for you today.

17

Living Simple

> "In all your ways, know and acknowledge and recognize Him, And He will make your paths straight and smooth [removing obstacles that block your way]."
>
> PROVERBS 3:6 *AMP*

Simple, pure, clear, humble

Busy, occupied, crowded, hectic

Jesus lived a simple life, so why shouldn't we? In a world where busy seems to portray success, ponder on what Jesus and living a simplified life would bring instead.

Do you feel you live a simple life or busy life?

_____

_____

_____

_____

_____

_____

_____

Do you feel it's right to be busy all the time?

_____

_____

_____

_____

_____

_____

Jesus called us to a simple way of life. I believe we miss a lot of what He wants for us, and speaks to us, by being busy.

Are you willing to look at your planner or schedule and ask Jesus to lead you? Are you willing to give up some busy for more time with Him and His will?

_____

_____

_____

_____

_____

_____

18

Boundaries

> *"Do you not fear Me?' says the Lord. 'Do you not tremble [in awe] in My presence? For I have placed the sand as a boundary for the sea. An eternal decree and a perpetual barrier beyond which it cannot pass. Though the waves [of the sea] toss and break, yet they cannot prevail [against the sand ordained to hold them back]; Though the waves and the billows roar, yet they cannot cross over [the barrier]. [Is not such a God to be feared?]"*

JEREMIAH 5:22 *AMP*

Boundary, limits, borders

Boundaries. We all need our boundaries. Boundaries are so important to live by with how God has called us to truly live. He set boundaries as He created this beautiful world. He wants us to set them too. I think boundaries change often as life goes on for each one of us. It's always good to reevaluate your priorities and schedules.

As the world calls us to be busy, Jesus calls us to rest. Go to Him and ask His will. Ask Him to help you set boundaries, as I know these boundaries bring me peace, love and joy. I must set boundaries on saying yes when I should be saying no. Some will serve at their church until they are ragged and ran and never sit to hear Jesus speak. Some will do and do for others and never do for themselves. Some will never say no to the hard things the world portrays as good. Some will go a lifetime running scared in their ways instead of stopping and hearing His will. I pray He speaks so clearly to you on boundaries. Boundaries have changed my life.

Do you have boundaries?

_____

_____

_____

_____

_____

_____

How do you think boundaries could help you?

_____

_____

_____

_____

_____

_____

Setting boundaries can be hard but ask your loving Father for help to see where your lack of boundaries may be misleading you.

Set a boundary today and feel the freedom when you choose to live this way.

19

Do you Trust His Timing?

> "Therefore, humble yourselves under the mighty hand
> of God, that He may exalt you in due time,"
>
> I PETER 5:6 *NKJV*

Time, moment, season, life, hour

In His time. In His due time. In His time, this shall pass. In His time, you ask? In His time, it will be done. No sooner, no later, His time shall be the perfect, most amazing time you see. His time, it's hard to wait. His time is my faith. His time will come, you will see. His time you will receive. His time. Have peace in His loving, perfect time today. Sometimes this is hard for me. I want His time to be now. I don't always trust His time. I don't always see His timing as good. I want it to be on my time. I want to control the timing. I want to not feel sick for this long. I want my child to be well and not endure this hardship. I want my dream to come to pass now and not another couple of years since He spoke it. I want all these things in my time, but my time is not the best time. I choose to trust His time.

❋ *Are you struggling today to trust His timing is best?*

_____

_____

_____

_____

_____

_____

❋ *Why?*

_____

_____

_____

_____

_____

_____

❋ *Why is it hard for you to wait?*

_____

_____

_____

_____

_____

_____

How can you choose to see His time is better, when you have to wait today? Is He showing you something in the waiting?

_____

_____

_____

_____

_____

_____

_____

Fasting

> "Samuel said, "Has the Lord as great a delight in burnt offerings and sacrifices? As in obedience to the voice of the Lord? Behold, to obey is better than sacrifice, And to heed [is better] than the fat of rams."
>
> 1 SAMUEL 15:22 *AMP*

Fasting, abstinence, self-denial, sacrifice

I really have a hard time fasting. I start out all good and intent saying, Lord I'm going to spend the next few days in prayer and fasting. The prayer part is more natural to me than fasting. The fasting and no fast food is HARD. So, day two comes along and my blood sugar drops. I have a horrible headache and you will find me in the fast-food drive thru taking a bite of ice-cream. I look up, smile, and say Lord, obedience is better than sacrifice, and drive away shaking my head. For real though, thank God it's not our acts, and thank God for grace. Thank God, He sees and knows our hearts. Sometimes I can fast for a week, sometimes I make it for two days, but He knows my heart and my praise. Fasting is so good! Fasting moves mountains and heals. If you find yourself trying to fast in the beginning, don't be so hard on yourself. Try again.

Do you fast often?

_____

_____

_____

Why do you fast?

_____

_____

_____

_____

_____

What does the Bible say about fasting?

_____

_____

_____

_____

_____

I encourage everyone to fast. Ask the Lord to help you. I believe it brings you closer to Him when you do.

21

Do it Anyway

> *"Whatever I command you, be careful to observe it;*
> *you shall not add to it nor take away from it."*
>
> DEUTERONOMY 12:32 *NKJV*

Do, carry out, achieve, complete

Do it anyway. People will gossip. They will speak ill of you. Your family, friends and foes won't be for you. They will disagree with you. Do it anyway. Be you. Be who God called you to be. Be you. Have peace with God and be you. Don't worry about the haters and the chatters. Silence them out and be you. Be you and smile as you do.

Is there something you have been called to do but aren't doing out of fear of what others will say or do?

_____

_____

_____

_____

_____

_____

_____

_____

_____

How can you overcome this fear and do what God has called you to do today?

_____

_____

_____

_____

_____

_____

_____

_____

_____

I pray strength and courage for you today to overcome in praise.

22

Do you consider yourself a disciple?

"And when He had called His twelve disciples to Him, He gave them power over unclean spirits, to cast them out, and to heal all kinds of sickness and all kinds of disease. Now the names of the twelve apostles are these: first, Simon, who is called Peter, and Andrew his brother; James the son of Zebedee, and John his brother; Philip and Bartholomew; Thomas and Matthew the tax collector; James the son of Alphaeus, and Lebbaeus, whose surname was Thaddaeus; Simon the Cananite, and Judas Iscariot, who also betrayed Him. These twelve, Jesus sent out and commanded them, saying: "Do not go into the way of the Gentiles, and do not enter a city of the Samaritans. But go rather to the lost sheep of the house of Israel. And as you go, preach, saying, 'The kingdom of heaven is at hand.' Heal the sick, cleanse the lepers, raise the dead, cast out demons. Freely you have received, freely give. Provide neither gold, nor silver, nor copper in your money belts, nor bag for your journey, nor two tunics, nor sandals, nor staffs; for a worker is worthy of his food."

MATTHEW 10:1-10 *NKJV*

Disciple, follower, believer

12 disciples. They chose to follow Jesus. They believed in Him. They were not perfect. They all had their faults and findings. They were all very different. They loved Jesus. They wanted to share the gospel. Some doubted, one betrayed but most followed and obeyed. He called and chose each one of them. He called the humble and lowly. He taught them to go out and preach the gospel, to heal and prophesy. He loved them all very much and believed in them. He knew everything about them, and still chose them. So, let Him do the choosing and we do the loving.

What ways are you walking out being a disciple?

_____

_____

_____

_____

_____

_____

How can you do better?

_____

_____

_____

_____

_____

_____

» *If you are not, do you yearn to be? Ask Him today.*

_____

_____

_____

_____

_____

_____

_____

_____

_____

23

A mighty God we serve

> "The clouds poured down rain; the thunder rumbled
> in the sky. Your arrows of lightning flashed."
>
> PSALMS 77:17 *NLT*

Mighty, powerful, strong

I love a good rain, a good flood, a good storm. I love the lightning and thunder too. I love all these mysterious ways You show Yourself true. I love a good storm as it rolls through. I love knowing and honoring a God that sees it through, a God that commands it to start and to stop. I love you, God, that You are over the top.

Do you ever sit through these storms and ponder on how He commands them to start and stop?

Does it show His majesty to you in a new way?

Are you honored to serve and love a God that has this much power but still chose to create and love you?

24

What's your Thorn?

> "Because of the surpassing greatness and extraordinary nature of the revelations [which I received from God], for this reason, to keep me from thinking of myself as important, a thorn in the flesh was given to me, a messenger of Satan, to torment and harass me—to keep me from exalting myself!"
>
> 2 CORINTHIANS 12:7 *AMP*

Thorn, annoyance, trial, torment

What's your thorn? What's your annoyance that won't go away? What's your trial? What's that one thing you have asked for Him to take away but still lingers on? That thing that still shows up when you prayed it gone. What's your thorn? I ask for mine to be removed! I plead, Lord, I will never grow prideful and arrogant, it's true! If only You will take this away. As I sit today, I realize that's a promise I can't make. So, I will

60

praise You for this thorn, as I know I will remain humble, and I will live knowing You give and You take.

Why do you think He allows these thorns?

_____
_____
_____
_____
_____
_____

How can you praise Him in these trials?

_____
_____
_____
_____
_____
_____

Would you choose another way or endure this pain as He sees this is the way?

_____
_____
_____
_____
_____
_____

25

Guilt and Pressure

> "Beloved, if our heart does not convict us [of guilt],
> we have confidence [complete assurance and boldness]
> before God;"
>
> 1 JOHN 3:21 *AMP*

Guilt, remorse, blame, wrong

Pressure, stress, force, weight

Guilt and pressure go hand and hand. I've felt and I've been dealt. I hate missing my child's softball games. I hate getting a text at work saying, Mom when are you going to be home? The guilt rises. Am I enough? Am I doing enough? Am I there enough? Am I the best mother I can be? I want to control it and everything. I want to be everywhere even if it means losing my peace. I don't want to ever let those two girls down. But maybe

I am not. Maybe I am showing them, and teaching them, and loving them, and praying for them not to lose. I am showing them it can't all be done. I am showing them how to be strong in letting go. I am showing them that God knows. He knows best and how to handle our stress and cares. We have to give them to Him and live there. So, maybe it's the enemy's scheme to make you believe... I hear the Lord say, let go and be set free. You can't do it all and that's okay.

How do you handle guilt?

_____
_____
_____
_____
_____

Do you feel pressure situations a lot?

_____
_____
_____
_____

How can you let go today?

_____
_____
_____
_____
_____

He wants to set us free, seek our King on your knees.

26

Pride and Jealousy

> "For where envy and self-seeking exist, confusion and every evil thing are there."
>
> JAMES 3:16 *NKJV*

> "By pride comes nothing but strife, but with the well-advised is wisdom."
>
> PROVERBS 13:10 *NKJV*

Jealousy, envy, spite, rivalry, Pride, arrogance

Jealousy and pride are so destructive. They may seem like small things in the natural, but in the spiritual they wreak havoc on relationships and on self. Woe to the prideful one that comes against in strife and arrogance. Be humble in these attacks and wisdom shall follow you. For the jealous and self-seeking, who are you trying to please? Who are you in competition with? These spirits are evil and will cause division and confusion. Woe to these things. When these spirits rise up against, go low, be humble and repent. Our wisdom is our defense.

Are you jealous?

_____

_____

_____

_____

Do you find yourself rearing up with pride?

_____

_____

_____

_____

These two things are so destructive. Ask the Lord to search your heart today. Ask Him to take these feelings away.

Challenge Your Thoughts

> *"casting down arguments and every high thing that exalts itself against the knowledge of God, bringing every thought into captivity to the obedience of Christ,"*
>
> **II CORINTHIANS 10:5** *NKJV*

Challenge, question, Thoughts, ideas, opinions

Challenge your thoughts. Don't take them all in and store them. Challenge them. Do they edify or encourage? Do they leave you hanging or lingering on? How do your thoughts make you feel? Do you find yourself, hours later, hopeless, mad or insecure? Do you find yourself in a pit of worry and anxiousness or in deep fear?

Challenge your thoughts today. Make them obey. Take control. Ask the Lord to help you filter these thoughts. Ask Him today. Don't waste another day bowing down to wrong thinking. Go to Him and start speaking, commanding the thoughts to obey, and see how your life can truly change.

If you are like me, one thought could lead me into anxiety. One thought, not taking captive, can lead me into a pit in a day. One bad thought leads to another, and I find myself in worry or in hate. Ask God to help you today to change.

Do you let your thoughts take over?

_____

_____

_____

_____

_____

How can you stop them?

_____

_____

_____

_____

_____

_____

_____

* *How can you train yourself to do better when these thoughts come back again and again?*

_____

_____

_____

_____

_____

_____

_____

_____

_____

_____

Meditate on His word and be intent today. It's a battle but you can win with Him.

28

Your Conscience and Confidence

> "For the Lord will be your confidence, firm and strong, and will keep your foot from being caught [in a trap]."
>
> PROVERBS 3:26 *AMP*

Conscience. Morals. Mind. Ethics.

Inner voice. Standards.

Confidence. Trust. Faith. Assurance. Belief.

I was listening to a Pastor teaching on, is your conscience blocking your confidence? That really made me think. I have never even put those two together. Is my conscience rooted in His word? Am I not obeying His commands? What about my standards? Are they set too high or too low? Do I let my mind wander out of control? Am I allowing that inner voice to speak to me daily? That's going to really affect my confidence in a good or bad way. Am I trusting and having faith in the word He speaks? Am I living a life of assurance and belief that our God is over everything? This definitely has me in check. We can't fully fulfill our calling if we aren't confident to do so. I pray for anyone struggling with confidence as I do sometimes. I pray you are led from the God that goes before His children and knows it all before we will even walk through it. We are blessed people when we know the truth.

Are you a confident person?

_____

_____

_____

Do you find your confidence in God?

_____

_____

_____

_____

How can you be more confident to walk in your calling?

_____

_____

_____

_____

_____

_____

29

What's your Mindset?

> *"In your relationships with one another, have the same mindset as Christ Jesus:"*
>
> PHILIPPIANS 2:5 *NIV*

Mindset, attitude, outlook

Oh, to have the same mindset as Jesus Christ. The same attitude. The same way of thinking. How would living be if you never had to fight the enemy with your thoughts? If your flesh bowed down and never reared up in sin. How would it be? This seems heavenly to me. Lord, help us be like You. Help us live humbly and in truth. Help us take every thought captive to obey and not let them linger on and stay. Oh, how I would love to have this daily. Teach us, show us, love us, lead us with the mindset that You have. Forever and ever, we shall be glad.

Do you long to truly be like Jesus?

_____

_____

_____

_____

_____

_____

Do you think this is hard in the world we live in?

_____

_____

_____

_____

_____

_____

Do you believe we can ask for His mindset and He will bless us with it?

_____

_____

_____

_____

_____

_____

30

How still are you?

> "Be still and know (recognize, understand) that I am God. I will be exalted among the nations! I will be exalted in the earth.""
>
> PSALMS 46:10 *AMP*

Still, silent, calm, unmoving

Is it hard to be still? To sit and feel His presence? In a world of busy, this is possible, but we have to be intent. Is it worth the peace you feel when you do? Or maybe a word He speaks when you sit still and hear His truth. It's worth it to me. I find myself thinking in the future a lot, the next softball game or night at dance or all these end of school activities. Maybe it's work and all the unknowns. My mind seems to be thinking of tomorrow or the to dos. Maybe you are living in the past. The mistakes, the hurt, the should have been. When I take my mind captive and say, be still, let's live for now, for today, for this next breath, oh, the peace it brings. We should be living in joy and thanksgiving. Let's not miss. Lord, help us all live in the now, the today, as we do not know our very last day.

❋ *Is it hard to be still?*

❋ *Why do you think He asks us to be still?*

❋ *Do you find peace in His presence?*

Is rest hard for you?

> *"Take My yoke upon you and learn from Me, for I am gentle and lowly in heart, and you will find rest for your souls."*
>
> MATTHEW 11:29 *NKJV*

Rest. Remain. Pause. Break.

Rest is so important for us. Why do we go months without rest? Do you feel lazy or worthless if you rest? Do you feel a void like something is missing if you don't keep yourself busy all the time? Does it hit your pride when all others have a full schedule ahead and you pencil in a day to rest? Maybe you are resting your body but not your mind. Maybe you are resting your heart but not your soul. Resting, oh resting, this I know. As I sit today and rest, I am so very blessed. I remember the days I wouldn't rest and I would run myself ragged and worn.

Do you know real rest?

_____

_____

_____

_____

_____

_____

Is it hard to rest?

_____

_____

_____

_____

_____

_____

If so, why?

_____

_____

_____

_____

_____

_____

Today, find some time and rest, or maybe take a few hours this week and rest. You will find yourself very blessed in your loving Fathers rest.

32

The reverential fear of the Lord

> "The [reverent] fear of the Lord [that is, worshiping
> Him and regarding Him as truly awesome] is the
> beginning and the preeminent part of knowledge
> [its starting point and its essence]; But arrogant fools
> despise [skillful and godly] wisdom and instruction
> and self-discipline."
>
> PROVERBS 1:7 *AMP*

Reverent, respect, honor

Having reverential fear of the Lord sounded unappealing to me. I didn't understand it. I thought wow, that sounds like something I don't want to sign up for. I lived life my way, I sinned, I lived in my own carnal knowledge. I always say sinning is fun until it's NOT. I loved doing things my way because I loved control.

As you see in this passage, I was labeled a fool. Who wants to be labeled as a fool? That day, I read this scripture in a new way. That day, I chose to give up myself and chose to fear the Lord. Wow, what a day.

The fear of the Lord means you respect and honor Him. It means you choose to serve Him and not the things of this world. Is it still hard some days? Of course. The fear of the Lord is the beginning of knowledge. Seek Him and let Him direct your ways. Put your hope, confidence and trust in Him. This is the starting point to a much, much better way.

Are you full of knowledge and wisdom fearing the Lord?

_____

_____

_____

_____

_____

_____

_____

How can you choose to seek Him instead of yourself and the worlds way?

_____

_____

_____

_____

_____

_____

_____

How do you think honoring the Lord blesses you?

_____

_____

_____

_____

_____

_____

_____

_____

_____

I pray if this is your first-time yearning to really choose to fear the Lord, He comes with love and truth as you seek Him. I believe you will be blessed abundantly.

33

Are you living as a fool or choosing victory?

> *"Where there is no [wise, intelligent] guidance, the people fall [and go off course like a ship without a helm], But in the abundance of [wise and godly] counselors there is victory."*
>
> PROVERBS 11:14 *AMP*

Fool, mislead

Victory, triumph, success, advantage, prosperity

I said before, this isn't always easy. It's a lifestyle change. It's going against the world and its ways. We live in this world, so it takes being intent in the word, and daily, sometimes hourly, choosing Him. It is possible, and when you fail, He's still there. He has forgiving grace that takes no other place. You can always go back to Him. Choose victory today. Reject the counsel by the ones that aren't honoring God. Choose the counsel that won't lead you astray. Choose Him today.

Who are you listening to?

_____

_____

_____

_____

_____

_____

_____

If it's not Godly wisdom, how does this work out for you?

_____

_____

_____

_____

_____

_____

_____

_____

✳ *Do you believe true victory in your life comes from the Lord's guidance and wisdom?*

✳ *How can you choose His guidance daily even when it's hard?*

34

Bind them upon your Heart.

> *"Bind them continually upon your heart (in your thoughts), and tie them around your neck."*
>
> PROVERBS 6:21 *AMP*

Bind, attach, join, secure

Heart, core, center, soul, spirit

Bind them upon your heart, soul, and mind. When you choose to fear the Lord and live this way, you will reap the most amazing knowledge, wisdom, guidance, counsel, and way. We are the blessed ones. We get to bind this beautiful powerful word upon our hearts and thoughts. We are blessed. We will flourish greatly in every aspect of our life. We are blessed in this great way as it guides our course. We are blessed friends, so very blessed. There is no better way.

How can you thank God for His great knowledge and guidance today?

_____

_____

_____

_____

_____

_____

How can you continue this daily for the rest of your life?

_____

_____

_____

_____

_____

_____

_____

Do you have a circle, person, or mentor that can keep you seeking this path?

_____

_____

_____

_____

_____

If you don't already have someone, or a few, ask God to bring these special ones into your life to encourage and edify you.

35

Do you trust God?

> *"Trust in and rely confidently on the Lord with all your heart. And do not rely on your own insight or understanding."*
>
> PROVERBS 3:5 *AMP*

Trust, faith, believe, confidence, hope, expectancy

It's easy to say, I trust Him. Do I rely confidently, most times. I may struggle within moments of distress. Mostly, when my own insight and understanding take over and the control of planning and wanting to know things now. My way. Yeah, I can trust but in the hard, hard times, but when the battle has been long, I don't always do this well. I take the lead and my heart can tell. I grow weary, lost, and confused. I'm tormented, emotional, and feel abused. I get into this funk, and honestly, I don't mind staying there for a while because it's nice to not have to fight. It's easy sometimes to sit in pity. Oh, but joy comes in the morning. I know this really isn't right to sit and loathe so, I wake up and tell the lover of my soul to take hold. I repent. I sit and praise Him for His goodness and slowly the fog leaves and I can finally see.

Do you have a hard time trusting God?

_____

_____

_____

_____

_____

_____

Do you rely on Him with your whole heart?

_____

_____

_____

_____

_____

_____

What makes it easy to trust?

_____

_____

_____

_____

_____

_____

What makes it hard?

_____

_____

_____

_____

_____

Write down as many times as you can, I trust you, Lord. I trust Your plans.

_____

_____

_____

_____

_____

_____

_____

_____

_____

Understand little. Trust much. Understand. Comprehend. Figure out little. Trust. Rely. Believe much. Don't worry your head. Don't worry your heart. Your health is more than those darts. Don't worry your head. Don't worry you heart. Don't go along just to fall apart. Don't worry your head, don't worry your heart. Trust Him with everything. That's your start.

36

Pressure and Pain

> "For at that time there will be a great tribulation (pressure, distress, oppression), such as has not occurred since the beginning of the world until now, nor ever will [again]."
>
> MATTHEW 24:21 *AMP*

Pressure, force, strain, stress, tension

Pain, hurt, distress, suffering, torment, agony

Do you feel the stress and strain, tension and force in trials? Do you feel the hurt and suffering, torment and agony, in your deepest pain? I have and I do. I often have asked to take this excruciating trial away. I have learned to pray instead of asking it away. Why? Maybe because this is our growth and gains for the coming day? Maybe, just maybe, this is the strength we have to fight. If we never faced a trial, a battle, would we be prepared for the end times when our messiah comes back? Would we be able to stand firm until the very end? I know I wouldn't have the strength if it was always easy.

What has been your deepest pain that God has seen you through?

_____

_____

_____

_____

_____

_____

_____

How can you praise Him in your trials now that you know these trials actually prepare you for your journey ahead?

_____

_____

_____

_____

_____

_____

Thank Him for the strength, character built, growth, and gains today.

Pressure. Tension. Uneasy. Stress. Do you ever feel the pressure to measure up? The pressure of the here, right now? The pressure of someone waiting on you? The pressure of life's problems? The pressure of the whole world on your shoulders? The pressure can feel like a ton of bricks. The pressure can feel like a kick. The pressure comes on so quick. The pressure can feel like an anxiety attack. A loved one not holding back. The pressure you feel is real. But, as children of God we have a better way to deal. Take a deep breath and take the pressure off by going to Him and letting Him have it all. Sit and say, Jesus have it your way today, take this pressure and stay.

37

Let go

Let go, release, loosen, free

What are you holding on so tightly to? Is it sin that needs bind loose? Is it your child that won't forgive you? Is it what you say or what you do? Is it the guilt that overtakes you? Is it shame, so you choose to remain? Is it hurt and deep pain? What won't you release? Is it insecurity? What do you need to be set free?

Letting go sounds so easy. Sounds so pleasing. Letting go can be in prayer. Letting go could mean giving it up for the last time. Letting go could be stopping your mind. Letting go could mean giving up. Letting go could mean you're tired of being stuck. Whatever it means for you today, ask the Lord to help you in a new way. Ask for forgiveness and repent. He's there waiting, so loosen your grip.

✳ *Write down what you need to let go of today.*

_____

_____

_____

_____

_____

_____

_____

_____

Ask Him to take it.

Fully give it to Him.

Smile. Breathe. Smile. Breathe.

Let go and be free.

38

Does lonely ever come?

Lonely, forgotten, withdrawn, empty

There have been times in my life when I have been surrounded
by people but felt I was the loneliest one in the room. There have
been places where I sat there wishing I could feel a connection,
but left with rejection. There have been hard seasons of growth
when I felt God called me from those friend groups. That was
lonely. I felt left out and forgotten. I felt sad and I mourned those
relationships I had built for years.

You could have all the money in the world and still be lonely. You could have everything you ever dreamed of, and the next hour feel lonely. If we aren't looking to Him as our true source, we will be lonely. I naturally love to be alone. This is a good thing for me, but also, I have allowed myself in seasons to withdraw so much from people that fellowship started to feel awkward. I have been deeply hurt so I didn't want to open up to anyone new. I think we have to be careful with this, especially if you are a loner.

The enemy loves to isolate you. If he can isolate you, he can find ways to attack, and you may end up alone in a pit. God created us for relationship. He promises us He will never leave or forsake us. He will never lose His grip on us. Friend, there may be times lonely hits, but smile, for He is always with.

Lonely won't kill you. It will grow you.

Seek Gods presence.

Ask the Holy Spirit to comfort you.

If today you feel lonely, why do you?

_____

_____

_____

_____

_____

_____

_____

_____

What has gotten you through feeling lonely in the past?

Hey, Jesus, it's me talking here. Where do You go when I'm lonely and scared? I hear Him say, I'm right here, surrender to Me and cast those cares.

39

Weary momma

"Are you weary, carrying a heavy burden? Come to me. I will refresh your life, for I am your oasis."

MATTHEW 11:28 *TPT*

Weary, exhausted
Momma, Grandmother, parent

To the weary momma who hasn't showered in days. To the weary momma that lost her praise. To the weary momma that chooses not to lose. To the weary momma that never takes time for you. To the weary momma who has changed 20 diapers today. To the weary momma that never rested but kept going to see another day. To the weary momma that sees nobody showing up. To the weary momma that feels lost in this season you are in. To the weary momma that smiles when feeling defeated. To the weary momma who doesn't say no. To the weary momma always offering their hand to hold. To the weary momma that nods her head when others say you will miss this.

It's ok to feel how you're feeling. Weary momma, it's ok to not be perfect. It's ok to lose your grip. It's ok to cry and say I'm done with all of it. Weary momma, it's ok to feel. Weary momma, you aren't the only one feeling this way. Weary momma, stretch your faith. Weary momma, God sees you where you are at. Weary momma, He chose you for the hardest task. Weary momma, one day those kids will look at you and thank you for all those weary days they have seen you go through.

These weary days can seem so overwhelming and so long. How do you deal with this kind of weariness?

_____

_____

_____

_____

_____

_____

Lack of sleep leads me into an emotional state on another level. How can you seek help for more rest?

_____

_____

_____

_____

_____

How do you feel when you have reached past the point of exhaustion?

_____

_____

_____

_____

_____

_____

Make time to sit each morning. If you have one minute or one hour, pray and ask Jesus to stay all day.

What are some rewards with being a momma? Write them down. You can have them in front of you for those hard, hard days to see you through.

_____

_____

_____

_____

_____

_____

_____

_____

_____

_____

_____

_____

_____

40

Sickness

"O Lord my God, I cried to you for help, and you restored my health."

PSALMS 30:2 *NLT*

"My wound is severe, and my grief is great. My sickness is incurable, but I must bear it."

JEREMIAH 10:19 *NLT*

Sickness, disease, infection, ill health

The two previous verses show two ways He answers. Sometimes He heals quickly, sometimes days, sometimes weeks, some endure for years, and some a lifetime. Why, I wonder? I would never really question that He knows. He sees the whole picture.

If I'm honest, sometimes it's hard and seems unfair. It may be sickness in your body. It may be sickness in your mind. It could be a disease that shows up one day and gone the next scan. Whatever reason one lives, and one dies, I will never understand. I battle with sickness a lot. I often want to question, why me God? I have learned to keep my hope in healing but also ok with praising Him through it. There is something about coming out stronger on the other side. Keeping me humble and not bursting with pride. If this is you today, keep your faith. It could change in a second for you if He commands. And if He doesn't, He is still good.

What type of sickness have you or do you currently deal with?

Do you believe in His healing and even miracles?

_____

_____

_____

_____

_____

_____

_____

Do you get angry at God when you don't understand His plans?

_____

_____

_____

_____

_____

_____

_____

Cry out to Him today, plead your case and have the faith.

When I'm sick, when I'm in defeat, when prayers aren't answered quickly. When I cry, when I fear, Father, help me not see these cares. As I go to my knees, look up above, bow down to the Father of love, something changes, something shifts. You, Father, only give life and life to the fullest. Healings, miracles, and all your goodness. Even though I endure hard times, never shall I miss that the timing is Yours. I shall wait for the day You call us home and this world, this sickness, will be no more.

41

Wherever He leads

Lead, guide, direct

Does the Lord ever lead you in ways you never thought? Has He called you out of a situation, relationship, school, workplace, sports team, church, event, season, but it's hard to leave because it's familiar and feels safe? Has He asked you to leave when you wanted to stay? Do you worry about the unknown? Has He asked you to rely on your faith? Has He? Does it feel like a struggle and too far to jump?

When you know, like you know the other side, you have won? He will lead you if you let Him. You have to choose. Will you live for Him or live for you? There have been many times He has called myself or my family out of our comfort zones, and every time I've seen Him on His throne. Every time, we have been blessed in that season. Every time, I have seen the why and the good. Every time, we say yes and surrender, we trust we will see Him do it again.

Do you allow God to lead you in everything?

_____
_____
_____
_____
_____
_____
_____
_____
_____

If yes, why is this hard sometimes?

_____
_____
_____
_____
_____
_____
_____
_____
_____
_____
_____

If you haven't had the courage yet, will you say yes to Him today?

_____

_____

_____

_____

_____

_____

_____

_____

_____

He is good. His ways are not our ways. He sees everything as we see a small picture. He loves us and wants us to succeed.

Declare you will trust Him over your life and everything. Surrender your will and your plans and watch how He leads.

42

Be Kind and Show Love

> *"Be kindly affectionate to one another with brotherly
> love, in honor giving preference to one another;"*
>
> ROMANS 12:10 *NKJV*

Kind, compassionate, gentle

Love, adore, devotion

My husband often tells me, you never know what someone is
going through. I have the kindest soul of a friend that preaches
and teaches her children to be kind, and they are, because she
is the most precious example. I am so blessed that my children
have them as friends.

A lot of times I find myself in my own way, thinking me, me, me, when the battle has been long. I believe it's only me who is going through all these things. It's not.

We all have something. We may try to hide it or downplay how we are handling things, but deep down we carry it, and we don't always release. So be kind. Love. Love the unlovable, they need it most. Don't be selfish. Smile and be glad. We have a Father who has our backs. You never know what one smile or act could do for someone. Who knows, you may be the only one that shines truth. You may be the only one that Jesus is seen through. Don't doubt the small things, to someone else it may be everything.

Are you naturally a kind person?

Do you get into selfish pits? I find when I do, if I go do something for another person in prayer or an act of kindness I instantly feel better.

How do you love the unlovable?

_____

_____

_____

_____

_____

_____

_____

_____

_____

Why do you think God calls us to live this way?

_____

_____

_____

_____

_____

_____

_____

_____

_____

43

The Gifts of the Spirit

> "for to one is given the word of wisdom through the Spirit, to another, the word of knowledge through the same Spirit, to another, faith by the same Spirit, to another, gifts of healings by the same Spirit, to another, the working of miracles, to another, prophecy, to another, discerning of spirits, to another, different kinds of tongues, to another, the interpretation of tongues. But one and the same Spirit works all these things, distributing to each one individually as He wills."
>
> I CORINTHIANS 12:8-11 *NKJV*

These are precious gifts. I remember before I would yearn for earthly gifts more than these. I didn't know any better really. The earthly gifts I can see. As I still love a good gift, once I experienced the spiritual gifts given by the Holy Spirit, wow just wow, how much more I enjoy these! They hit differently. They are everlasting, where the world's gifts fade away. I have something everlasting now that encourages, edifies, and blesses more than I could ever imagine. Also, these gifts you are to share. I am so blessed when these are shared by another follower, with me.

In the next days, we will go over each gift. Before we do, ask the Holy Spirit to reveal to you why He wants us to have these gifts and ask Him for the gifts today.

Word of Wisdom • Word of knowledge • Faith
Healing • Miracles • Prophecy • Discerning of Spirits
Tongues • Interpretation of Tongues

44

Word of wisdom

> *"Words of wisdom are like a fresh, flowing brook—like deep waters that spring forth from within, bubbling up inside the one with understanding."*
>
> PROVERBS 18:4 *TPT*

Wisdom, understanding, discernment

Wisdom. Thank God for wisdom. So many times before in my life, before walking in the gift of wisdom, I would question a lot. It was so hard to make a decision. Even if it was an easy one. The hard ones would take me out.

Now I get this unction, this feeling from the Holy Spirit quickly, and I am not of lack on decision making. He makes clear paths, He guides, He provides all the answers I will ever need. I just need to sit at His feet. I need to bow and surrender. It's all right there for the taking, and by this wisdom, I live every day in peace knowing He only gives the best to me.

Do you find it hard to get clear answers on decision making?

_____
_____
_____
_____
_____
_____

Do you believe God has all the answers?

_____
_____
_____
_____
_____
_____

Fill your mind with scripture, yield to the Holy Spirit today and ask Him to make you wise beyond your years.

_____
_____
_____
_____
_____
_____

45

Word of knowledge

"To know [skillful and godly] wisdom and instruction;
To discern and comprehend the words of
understanding and insight,"

PROVERBS 1:2 *AMP*

Knowledge, understanding, wisdom

God speaks. I didn't really know this for a long period of my life. I mostly thought He spoke to pastors, and even at that, not at the deep level I found He truly speaks. Once I grasped and heard this for myself, it was all over from there. I constantly went after His heart and His word. I wanted to know as much as I could as fast as I could. I couldn't believe He loved me so much or would care so much to see me, to give me a word I desperately needed and to encourage me. He speaks through the word, your friends, a stranger off the street. He speaks.

Listen up. When He speaks, it will line up with His word. Dive deep into His word, ask for Him to speak a word to you. It's that small inner voice, that thought, or another person speaking into your life. We are so blessed, He speaks.

Thank Him for speaking to you.

_____

_____

_____

_____

_____

_____

Ask Him to give you a word of knowledge.

_____

_____

_____

_____

_____

_____

Enjoy this relationship with the Holy Spirit and this precious gift given to us.

_____

_____

_____

_____

_____

_____

46

Faith

> *"For we walk by faith, not by sight."*
>
> II CORINTHIANS 5:7 *NKJV*

Faith, trust, belief, hope

You cannot see trust, belief, or hope with your eye sight. Walk by faith, not by sight. We cannot see faith. We can believe, we can feel, we can dream, we can trust God. My mom is so faith filled. I kind of held on to her faith for a long time. She speaks things, dreams things, believes God will do things, and sometimes honestly, it goes way over my head like, what? I prayed for that kind of faith.

Let me tell you the hope and faith that He has given me has pushed me past many broken dreams and insecurities. This kind of faith keeps me grounded when the going gets tough.

This kind of faith keeps me holding on to the hope, not the once was. This kind of faith in God is how I choose to live, because without faith I'm dead to what all He did. The Noah faith to build an arc because it's going to rain. The faith that Jesus died and rose again. The faith that He will be back to take us to heaven one day. I want to live by this faith.

If you are like how I was, don't feel bad. Faith takes courage. Faith takes speaking things into existence, dreaming, believing, and never giving up hope. Let's be honest, in this world it's kind of hard to do. So, live by faith and not by sight and see how our precious Lord takes you higher in this life.

Ask for the gift of faith to be an overflow in your life.

Start by writing down some things you are hopeful for. Speak them over and over and build your faith today.

_____

_____

_____

_____

_____

Speak of the resurrection life.

_____

_____

_____

_____

47

Healing

> "Therefore, confess your sins to one another [your false steps, your offenses], and pray for one another, that you may be healed and restored. The heartfelt and persistent prayer of a righteous man (believer) is able to accomplish much [when put into action and made effective by God—it is dynamic and can have tremendous power]."
>
> JAMES 5:16 *AMP*

Healing, mend, restore

Healing, Jesus, an act of love. He loves us so much. He died on the cross so we would be free. Every sin and sickness were nailed to that tree. His blood shed covers us all. Nothing too big nor too small. He is a healing Father who loves to heal. Sometimes healing can come quick, some takes weeks, months and leaves us with unforgiveness. Never question what He is doing. Always choose to believe He has the best for you.

If you need healing in your body today, confess your sins to Him. Pray He heals you. Pray for someone else who needs healing as well.

Watch as He may be healing your heart first.

Do you believe that His heart is to heal us? Do you get frustrated when the healing doesn't come for you or a family member?

_____

_____

_____

_____

_____

Why do you think sometimes healing doesn't come when we want it to?

_____

_____

_____

_____

_____

Go and be healed in Jesus's mighty name today! Proclaim health in your mind, body and soul. Pray for others too. There is so much power in prayer.

48

Miracles

> "Then God added his witness to theirs. He validated
> their ministry with signs, astonishing wonders, all
> kinds of powerful miracles, and by the gifts of the
> Holy Spirit, which he distributed as he desired."
>
> HEBREWS 2:4 *TPT*

Miracles, wonders, supernatural

Miracles, signs, and wonders. Yes, He still does. Miracles happen every day. It doesn't have to be just one big thing. Look around with eyes to see. It's a miracle He lives inside thee. Miracles are given, and help us to believe, there is something greater than our eyes can see.

Thank Him today for the miracles He has already given you.

_____
_____
_____
_____
_____
_____
_____
_____
_____
_____
_____
_____

Ask Him to help you see more miracles to come.

49

Prophecy

Prophecy, sign, revelation, warning

Prophecy is one of my favorite gifts. Prophecy is a word spoken given by the Holy Spirit. Gods will. This gift is to encourage and edify the church. To reveal to believers', truth. It convicts. It is so amazing to hear a word directly from God. It's a key to unlock when you maybe feel stuck. It's love. He loves us so much He wants to guide and encourage us. He wants to speak truth to edify and convict us. He wants the best for us.

Have you ever experienced a prophetic word spoken over you?

If not, ask and be open to this amazing gift given. Yes, it may seem different, but I promise you will be so blessed by it.

We have a God that loves to speak to us. Receive it.

50

Discerning of Spirits

> *"But the natural [unbelieving] man does not accept
> the things [the teachings and revelations] of the Spirit
> of God, for they are foolishness [absurd and illogical]
> to him; and he is incapable of understanding them,
> because they are spiritually discerned and appreciated,
> [and he is unqualified to judge spiritual matters]."*
>
> 1 CORINTHIANS 2:14 *AMP*

*Discernment, sense, understanding, insight,
wisdom*

Thank God for discernment. Really, thank Him today. Sometimes discerning can be hard because I am a feeler, so I feel everything. I remember when this gift was first given. I was in an atmosphere with lots of evil, lack of love, dishonest crowds. I wanted to run. I could barely stand being in there. It was a ministry the Lord had called me to be a part of for a season, but it was too much at times. Lots of drugs, lost people, fake, greed, and hate came through those doors.

I'm glad I stayed and went through; it taught me a thing or two. Now, my discernment radar goes off in an instant, and then I feel like I'm on high alert of a situation or person. It's like, back up 10 feet please, before we proceed. As hard as this gift of feeling can be sometimes, I wouldn't trade it for anything. It has pushed me through lots of things like growth. It has helped me when I needed a key, an answer or truth. This gift truly blesses me.

Discernment is so important to have in this world. Ask for it. Trust, He will lead you through this life, guiding and protecting you.

Do you discern well?

_____

_____

_____

_____

If you do, is it hard sometimes on you?

_____

_____

_____

_____

_____

❈ What are the benefits of discernment?

_____
_____
_____
_____
_____
_____
_____
_____
_____

If you want better discernment, ask Him.

51

Tongues

Tongues, utterance, heavenly language

Hear me out. I know tongues can be weird. I used to freak out and think people were weird doing it. I never wanted to ask for this gift because I thought it was so weird. Once I did ask for it, I don't feel it came easy. Maybe because, again... deep down, I felt it was weird. After months of asking and wondering, one day it came. It was so simple it came in two words. It didn't make sense in the natural, but in my spirit, I felt it unlocked peace. It unlocked me thinking.

Often, we do not know how to truly pray for ourselves or others. Tongues is a great way because it is the Holy Spirit praying on our behalf. I don't use tongues nearly as often as I should. I know it's a big key for me. Maybe it's the enemy's way of keeping me from peace. Tongues confuses the enemy, so of course he wouldn't want us to speak them. I do have to say that when I'm troubled in anxiety, I will go straight to tongues, and also when my daughter is pitching on the mound, I use them a lot he he. It comforts me. Tongues are very edifying. Tongues are a good thing. Also, I believe tongues is a big key in casting out demons. He gives us power to do these things. Just believe.

Meditate on the word He has given us about speaking in tongues.

Ask the Holy Spirit to show you this heavenly language if you are yearning for it.

Be open. Don't let the past or whatever other opinions are stop you from this beautiful gift.

52

Interpretation of Tongues

> *"Therefore let him who speaks in a tongue pray that he may interpret."*
>
> I CORINTHIANS 14:13 *NKJV*

Interpretation, explanation, understanding

Yes, yes, yes. Pray to interpret what you are speaking. This has helped our small tribe tremendously. We can unlock and use this tongue for certain situations. We can get straight to the point and use as a powerful weapon to conquer anything trying keep us in bondage. Ask, ask, ask.

※ *Is interpreting tongues something your spirit longs for?*

This is a powerful gift. Ask and receive today.

※ *Write down the benefits of this gift and hold on to them.*

53

You are empowered to walk in these gifts

> "Now, there are [distinctive] varieties of spiritual gifts [special abilities given by the grace and extraordinary power of the Holy Spirit operating in believers], but it is the same Spirit [who grants them and empowers believers]."
>
> 1 CORINTHIANS 12:4 *AMP*

Empowered, authorized, enabled

Now that we have gone over all the gifts of the spirit, sit down, go back over each gift. Ask the Holy Spirit to dive in deeper.

Seek and find. Which gift or gifts are stirring inside of you? Go for them! Receive them. Thank Him for them. Enjoy these gifts as they are better than any worldly treasure here on earth. They outweigh everything. They are priceless, and He gives them to His children of faith.

I pray these gifts are lavished upon you in Jesus's name.

Don't forget to share them with others that may come your way.

Praise, praise, praise.

54

Love First

> "And if I were to have the gift of prophecy with a profound understanding of God's hidden secrets, and if I possessed unending supernatural knowledge, and if I had the greatest gift of faith that could move mountains, but have never learned to love, then I am nothing."
>
> 1 CORINTHIANS 13:2 *TPT*

> All these gifts are wonderful, but if you don't have love that stays, these gifts will eventually fade. "Jesus said to him, 'You shall love the Lord your God with all your heart, with all your soul, and with all your mind.' And the second is like it: 'You shall love your neighbor as yourself.'"
>
> MATTHEW 22:37, 39 *NKJV*

Always carry love in your back pocket. Keep it for those hard things. Always show love to the most unlovable. Live with a heart that chooses to love when loving is hard. Love the hurting. Love the poor in spirit. Love the church. Love the lost. Love your family and friends. Learn to love and speak kind words. Forgive the offense. Love does not disrespect or shame. Love is not selfish or easily irritated. Love and give. Be patient and gentle in love. Do not be jealous. God is love. Love never gives up.

Loving others can be hard to do. Below are two scriptures that help get myself in check when I'm not loving well.

"He who does not love does not know God, for God is love."

I JOHN 4:8 *NKJV*

"Our love for others is our grateful response to the love God first demonstrated to us."

1 JOHN 4:19 *TPT*

I want to love because I know God, and that convicts my heart reading it. I also want to love because God loved us first. Jesus on the cross. His sacrifice. His love. I want to love because He showed us the greatest love.

Is it hard to love at all times?

_____

_____

_____

_____

_____

_____

_____

Do you love your enemies?

_____

_____

_____

_____

_____

_____

Ask for a loving heart like Jesus's today.

Ask Him to show you and teach you ways to love when it's hardest to do so.

55

Jesus prayed for all to be One

"And I ask not only for these disciples, but also for all those who will one day believe in me through their message. I pray for them all to be joined together as one, even as You and I, Father, are joined together as one. I pray for them to become one with us so that the world will recognize that You sent me. For the very glory You have given to me I have given them so that they will be joined together as one and experience the same unity that we enjoy. You live fully in me, and now I live fully in them so that they will experience perfect unity, and the world will be convinced that You have sent me, for they will see that You love each one of them with the same passionate love that You have for me."

JOHN 17:20-23 *TPT*

Unity, union, accord, oneness, agreement, wholeness, peace, working together

They will know we are Christians by our love, comes to mind. If we as believers can't come together as one in love, what are we showing the unbelievers? Jesus prayed. His heart was for us all to be one. He is one with His Father. We are now one in Him. My heart is for the whole church to be one. All the religions and denominations to love each-other without division because of standards or the way they do things differently. If we all agree Christ died for us as we were still sinners, how can we not agree to love one another as believers in Christ? I see so much division and hurt and my heart cries out, Father, let us all be one. Let us all be in union and declare your precious name together. Let no walls divide us. Let our hearts become one in You, Lord. Drop all the fear and insecurities the enemy has placed upon us and his lies to divide us. We stand up and say we are one because that is Your heart Jesus.

Pray today for the church to be one in Jesus. To show love. To be love. To proclaim His name above all names. We pray unity. We pray the enemy holds no ground. We pray we are victorious heirs of the one true king, and we believe in Jesus mighty name. Amen.

Acknowledgments

About the Author

I believe it's the Father, the Son, and the Holy Ghost, and everything else flows from it. I have an amazing husband, Justin, of sixteen years. I have two precious daughters that make my world go round. Addie, 14 and Liv, 9. We reside in Bourbon, MO and founded True Love Ministries.

My heart is to flow from the heart of Jesus and tell the world the relationship with our Father is the most important of all.

CPSIA information can be obtained
at www.ICGtesting.com
Printed in the USA
JSHW052003151122
33258JS00003B/17

9 781959 608028